Testing Vue.js Components with Jest

A concise guide to testing Vue.js components using Jest and the official Vue Test Utils library

Alex Jover Morales

Testing Vue.js Components with Jest

Copyright © 2019 Packt Publishing

Author: Alex Jover Morales

Managing Editor: Ashish James

Acquisitions Editor: Karan Wadekar

Production Editor: Salma Patel

Editorial Board: Bharat Botle, Ewan Buckingham, Megan Carlisle, Simon Cox, Mahesh Dhyani, Manasa Kumar, Alex Mazonowicz, Dominic Pereira, Shiny Poojary, Abhishek Rane, Erol Staveley, Ankita Thakur, Nitesh Thakur, and Jonathan Wray

First Published: October 2019

Production Reference: 1171019

ISBN: 978-1-83921-968-9

Published by Packt Publishing Ltd.

Livery Place, 35 Livery Street

Birmingham B3 2PB, UK

Table of Contents

Chapter 9: Snapshot Testing

Index

Preface

About

This section briefly introduces the author and what this book covers.

About the Book

Unit testing in modern component-based JavaScript frameworks is not straightforward. You need a test suite that is reliable and runs quickly. Components are connected to one another, and the browser adds a layer of UI, which makes everything inter-dependent while we test components in isolation. Jest is a fully-featured JavaScript testing framework that will do all your work for you.

This book shows you how to test Vue.js components easily and take advantage of the fully-featured Jest testing framework with the aid of practical examples. You'll learn the different testing styles and their structures. You'll also explore how your Vue.js components respond to various tests. You'll see how to apply techniques such as snapshot testing, shallow rendering, module dependency mocking, and module aliasing to make your tests smooth and clean.

By the end of this book, you'll know all about testing your components by utilizing the features of Jest.

About the Authors

Alex Jover Morales is a Vue.js core team partner. He co-organizes Alicante Frontend and Vue Day. He is an instructor at Alligatorio and is interested in web performance, PWA, code quality, and the human side of code.

Learning Objectives

- Set up a Vue-test project to get started with Jest
- Unit test your components using techniques such as shallow rendering
- Gain insights into how to test the reactive parts in the logic of the Vue.js components
- Explore how to test deeply rendered Vue.js components
- Perform easy and quick tests with module dependency mocking, module aliasing, and more
- Know-how and when to use snapshot testing

Audience

If you are a programmer looking to make your development process smooth and bug-free, this is an ideal book for you. Some prior knowledge and experience of JavaScript will help you quickly and easily grasp the concepts explained in this book.

Approach

This book uses easy-to-understand language to explain the various concepts of testing. With a perfect blend of theory and practice, it shows you how to test Vue.js components easily by utilizing the various features of Jest.

Write the First Vue.js Component Unit Test in Jest

The official VueJS testing library, **vue-test-utils** (https://github.com/vuejs/vue-test-utils), which is based on **avoriaz** (https://github.com/eddyerburgh/avoriaz), is just around the corner. Indeed, **@EddYerburgh** (https://twitter.com/EddYerburgh) is doing a very good job of creating it. This library provides all the necessary tooling to make writing unit tests in a VueJS application easy.

Jest (https://facebook.github.io/jest), on the other side, is a testing framework developed at Facebook, which makes testing a breeze using a number of awesome features, including the following:

- Almost no configuration by default
- A very cool interactive mode
- Running tests in parallel

- Testing with Spies, stubs, and mocks out of the box
- Built-in code coverage
- Snapshot testing
- Module-mocking utilities

You've probably already written tests without using any of these tools, just by using Karma, Mocha, Chai, Sinon, and so on, but you'll see how much easier it can be with these tools.

Setting Up a vue-test Sample Project

Let's start by creating a new project using **vue-cli** (https://github.com/vuejs/vue-cli) and answering NO to all yes/no questions:

```
npm install -g vue-cli
vue init webpack vue-test
cd vue-test
```

Then, we'll need to install some dependencies, as follows:

```
# Install dependencies
npm i -D jest vue-jest babel-jest
```

jest-vue-preprocessor (https://github.com/vire/jest-vue-preprocessor) is required to make Jest understand .**vue** files, and **babel-jest** (https://github.com/facebook/jest/tree/master/packages/babel-jest) is required for integration with Babel.

Now install 'vue-test-utils' library.

```
npm i -D @vue/test-utils
```

Let's add the following Jest configuration in the **package.json**:

```
{
  "jest": {
    "moduleNameMapper": {
      "^vue$": "vue/dist/vue.common.js"
    },
    "moduleFileExtensions": ["js", "vue"],
```

```
    "transform": {
      "^.+\\.js$": "<rootDir>/node_modules/babel-jest",
      ".*\\.(vue)$": "<rootDir>/node_modules/vue-jest"
    }
  }
}
```

moduleFileExtensions will tell Jest which extensions to look for, and **transform** will tell Jest which preprocessor to use for a file extension.

Finally, add a **test** script to the **package.json**:

```
{
  "scripts": {
    "test": "jest"
  }
}
```

Testing a Component

I'll be using single-file components here, and I haven't checked whether splitting them into their own **HTML**, **CSS**, or **js** files works or not, so let's assume you're doing that as well.

First, create a **MessageList.vue** component under **src/components**:

```
<template>
  <ul>
    <li v-for="message in messages">
      {{ message }}
    </li>
  </ul>
</template>

<script>
  export default {
    name: "list",
    props: ["messages"]
  };
</script>
```

And then update **App.vue** to use it as follows:

```
<template>
  <div id="app">
    <MessageList :messages="messages" />
  </div>
</template>

<script>
  import MessageList from "./components/MessageList";

  export default {
    name: "app",
    data: () => ({ messages: ["Hey John", "Howdy Paco"] }),
    components: {
      MessageList
    }
  };
</script>
```

We already have a couple of components that we can test. Let's create a **test** folder under the project root and an **App.test.js** file:

```
import Vue from "vue";
import App from "../src/App";

describe("App.test.js", () => => {
  let cmp, vm;

  beforeEach(() => => {
    cmp = Vue.extend(App); // Create a copy of the original component
    vm = new cmp({
      data: {
        // Replace data value with this fake data
        messages: ["Cat"]
      }
    }).$mount(); // Instances and mounts the component
  });

  it('equals messages to ["Cat"]', () => => {
    expect(vm.messages).toEqual(["Cat"]);
  });
});
```

Now, if we run **npm test** (or **npm t** as a shorthand version), the test should run and pass. Since we're modifying the tests, let's run it in **watch mode**:

```
npm t -- --watch
```

The Problem with Nested Components

This test is too simple. Let's check that the output is expected as well. For that, we can use the amazing Snapshot feature of Jest, which will generate a snapshot of the output and check it against the upcoming runs. Add after the previous **it** in **App.test.js**:

```
it("has the expected html structure", () => {
  expect(cmp.element).toMatchSnapshot();
});
```

This will create a **test/__snapshots__/App.test.js.snap** file. Let's open it and inspect it:

```
// Jest Snapshot v1, https://goo.gl/fbAQLP

exports['App.test.js has the expected html structure 1'] = '
<div id="app">
  <ul>
    <li>
      Cat
    </li>
  </ul>
</div>
';
```

If you don't know very much about Snapshot, don't worry; I'll cover it in more depth in *Chapter 9, Snapshot Testing*.

In case you haven't noticed, there is a big problem here: the **MessageList** component has been rendered as well. **Unit tests** must be tested as **independent units**, meaning that in **App.test.js**, we want to test the **App** component and not have to care about anything else at all.

This can be the cause of several problems. Imagine, for example, that the children components (**MessageList**, in this case) perform side-effect operations on the **created** hook, such as the calling of **fetch**, there being a Vuex action, or a change of state. That's something we definitely don't want.

Luckily, **shallow rendering** solves this nicely.

What Is Shallow Rendering?

Shallow rendering (http://airbnb.io/enzyme/docs/api/shallow.html) is a technique that ensures that your component is rendering without children. This is useful for:

- Testing only the component you want to test (that's what unit tests stand for)

- Avoiding side effects that children components can have, such as making HTTP calls, calling store actions, and so on

Testing a Component with Vue-Test-Utils

vue-test-utils provides us with shallow rendering, among other features. We could rewrite the previous test as follows:

```
import { shallowMount } from "@vue/test-utils";
import App from "../src/App";

describe("App.test.js", () => {
  let cmp;

  beforeEach(() => {
    cmp = shallowMount(App, {
      // Create a shallow instance of the component
      data: {
        messages: ["Cat"]
      }
    });
  });

  it('equals messages to ["Cat"]', () => {
    // Within cmp.vm, we can access all Vue instance methods
    expect(cmp.vm.messages).toEqual(["Cat"]);
  });

  it("has the expected html structure", () => {
    expect(cmp.element).toMatchSnapshot();
  });
});
```

And now, if you're still running Jest in **watch** mode, you'll see that the test still passes, but the Snapshot doesn't match. Press *u* to regenerate it. Then, open and inspect it again:

```
// Jest Snapshot v1, https://goo.gl/fbAQLP

exports['App.test.js has the expected html structure 1'] = '
<div id="app">
  <!--  -->
</div>
';
```

Do you see? Now, no children have been rendered and we tested the **App** component **fully isolated** from the component tree. Also, if you have any **created** or other hooks in the children's components, they haven't been called either.

If you're curious about *how shallow rendering is implemented*, check out the **source code** (https://github.com/vuejs/vue-test-utils/blob/dev/packages/test-utils/src/shallow-mount.js) and you'll see that it is basically stubbing the **components** key, the **render** method, and the life cycle hooks.

In the same vein, you can implement the **MessageList.test.js** test as follows:

```
import { mount } from '@vue/test-utils'
import MessageList from '../src/components/MessageList'

describe('MessageList.test.js', () => {
  let cmp

  beforeEach(() => {
    cmp = mount(MessageList, {
      // Be aware that props is overridden using 'propsData'
      propsData: {
        messages: ['Cat']
      }
    })
  })
```

```
})

it('has received ['Cat'] as the message property', () => {
  expect(cmp.vm.messages).toEqual(['Cat'])
})

it('has the expected html structure', () => {
  expect(cmp.element).toMatchSnapshot()
})
})
```

You can find the full example from this chapter on **GitHub** (https://github.com/alexjoverm/vue-testing-series/tree/lesson-1).

Test Deeply Rendered Vue.js Components

So far, we've seen how to use shallow rendering to test a component in isolation, preventing the component's sub-tree from rendering.

But in some cases, we want to test components that behave as a group, or **molecules** (http://atomicdesign.bradfrost.com/chapter-2/#molecules), as stated in *Atomic Design*. Keep in mind that this applies to **Presentational Components** (https://medium.com/@dan_abramov/smart-and-dumb-components-7ca2f9a7c7d0) since they're unaware of app state and logic. In most cases, you'd want to use shallow rendering for container components.

Adding a Message Component

In the case of **Message** and **MessageList** components, apart from writing their own individual unit tests, we might want to test them both as a unit as well.

Let's start by creating **components/Message.vue**:

```
<template>
  <li class="message">{{ message }}</li>
</template>

<script>
  export default {
    props: ["message"]
  };
</script>
```

And update **components/MessageList.vue** to use it:

```
<template>
  <ul>
    <Message :message="message" v-for="message in messages" />
  </ul>
</template>

<script>
  import Message from "./Message";

  export default {
    props: ["messages"],
    components: {
      Message
    }
  };
</script>
```

Testing MessageList with a Message Component

To test **MessageList** with deep rendering, we just need to use **mount** instead of **shallowMount** in the previously created **test/MessageList.test.js**:

```
import { mount } from "@vue/test-utils";
import MessageList from "../src/components/MessageList";

describe("MessageList.test.js", () => {
  let cmp;

  beforeEach(() => {
    cmp = mount(MessageList, {
      // Be aware that props is overridden using 'propsData'
      propsData: {
        messages: ["Cat"]
      }
    });
  });

  it('has received ["Cat"] as the message property', () => {
    expect(cmp.vm.messages).toEqual(["Cat"]);
  });

  it("has the expected html structure", () => {
    expect(cmp.element).toMatchSnapshot();
  });
});
```

By the way, have you noticed the **beforeEach** thing? That's a very clean way to create a clean component before each test, which is very important in unit testing since it defines that tests shouldn't depend on each other.

Both **mount** and **shallowMount** use exactly the same API; the difference is in the rendering. I'll progressively show you more of the API as we move along in this series.

If you run **npm t**, you'll see the test is failing because the Snapshot doesn't match **MessageList.test.js**. To regenerate it, run with the **-u** option:

```
npm t -- -u
```

Then, if you open and inspect **test/__snapshots__/MessageList.test.js.snap**, you'll see the **class="message"** is there, meaning the component has been rendered:

```
// Jest Snapshot v1, https://goo.gl/fbAQLP

exports['MessageList.test.js has the expected html structure 1'] = '
<ul>
  <li class="message">
    Cat
  </li>
</ul>
';
```

Keep in mind to avoid deep rendering when there could be side effects, since the children component hooks, such as **created** and **mount**, will be triggered, and there could be HTTP calls or other side effects there that we don't want to be called. If you want to try out what I'm saying, add a **console.log** to the **Message.vue** component, in the **created** hook:

```
export default {
  props: ["message"],
  created() {
    console.log("CREATED!");
  }
};
```

Then, if you run the tests again with **npm t**, you'll see the **"CREATED!"** text in the terminal output. So, be cautious.

You can find the code and examples for this chapter on **GitHub** (https://github.com/alexjoverm/vue-testing-series/tree/Test-fully-rendered-Vue-js-Components-in-Jest).

3

Test Styles and Structure

So far, we've tested using **Jest Snapshots** (https://facebook.github.io/jest/docs/snapshot-testing.html). In most cases, that's what we'll use, but sometimes we may want to assert something more specific.

Although you can access a Vue instance via `cmp.vm` (https://github.com/alexjoverm/vue-testing-series/blob/master/test/MessageList.test.js#L17), you have a set of utilities at your disposal to make it easier. Let's see what we can do.

The Wrapper Object

Wrapper is the main object of **vue-test-utils**. It is the type returned by the **mount**, **shallowMount**, **find**, and **findAll** functions. You can see the whole API and typings **here** (https://github.com/vuejs/vue-test-utils/blob/v1.0.0-beta.27/packages/test-utils/types/index.d.ts).

find and findAll

find and **findAll** accept a **selector** (https://github.com/vuejs/vue-test-utils/blob/v1.0.0-beta.27/packages/test-utils/types/index.d.ts#L92) as an argument, which can be a CSS selector and a Vue component as well.

So, we can do things such as:

```
let cmp = mount(MessageList);
expect(cmp.find(".message").element).toBeInstanceOf(HTMLElement);

// Or even call it multiple times
let el = cmp.find(".message").find("span").element;

// Although for the previous example, we could do it in one
let el = cmp.find(".message span").element;
```

Asserting Structure and Style

Let's add more tests to **MessageList.test.js**:

```
it("is a MessageList component", () => {
  expect(cmp.is(MessageList)).toBe(true);

  // Or with CSS selector
  expect(cmp.is("ul")).toBe(true);
});

it("contains a Message component", () => {
  expect(cmp.contains(Message)).toBe(true);

  // Or with CSS selector
  expect(cmp.contains(".message")).toBe(true);
});
```

Here, we're using **is** to assert the root component type and **contains** to check for the existence of sub-components. Just like **find**, they receive a Selector, which can be a CSS selector or component.

We have some utils to assert the **Vue instance**:

```
it("Both MessageList and Message are vue instances", () => {
  expect(cmp.isVueInstance()).toBe(true);
  expect(cmp.find(Message).isVueInstance()).toBe(true);
});
```

Now we're going to assert **structure** in more detail:

```
it("Message element exists", () => {
  expect(cmp.find(".message").exists()).toBe(true);
});

it("Message is not empty", () => {
  expect(cmp.find(Message).isEmpty()).toBe(false);
});

it('Message has a class attribute set to "message"', () => {
  expect(cmp.find(Message).attributes().class).toBe("message");
});
```

The **exists**, **isEmpty**, and **attributes** methods come in handy for this.

Then, we have **classes** and **attributes().style** to assert **styling**. Let's update the **Message.vue** component with a style, since **attributes().style** asserts only inline styles:

```
<li style="margin-top: 10px" class="message">{{message}}</li>
```

Here are the tests:

```
it("Message component has the .message class", () => {
  expect(cmp.find(Message).classes()).toContain("message");
});

it("Message component has style padding-top: 10", () => {
  expect(cmp.find(Message).attributes().style).toBe("padding-top: 10px;");
});
```

There is a bunch of utils to make testing Vue components easier. You can find them all in **the typings file** (https://github.com/vuejs/vue-test-utils/blob/v1.0.0-beta.27/packages/test-utils/types/index.d.ts).

You can find the working code of this chapter on **GitHub** (https://github.com/alexjoverm/vue-testing-series/blob/Test-Styles-and-Structure-in-Vue-js-and-Jest/test/MessageList.test.js).

Test Properties and Custom Events

There are different ways to test properties, events, and custom events.

Properties are custom attributes that are passed down from parent components to child components. Custom events do just the opposite: they send data out to the direct parent via an event. When they are combined, they are the wires of interaction and communication in Vue.js components.

In unit testing, testing the ins and outs (properties and custom events) means testing how a component behaves when it receives and sends out data in isolation. So, let's get our hands dirty.

Properties

When we are testing component properties, we can test how the component behaves when we pass it certain properties. However, before going on, consider this important note:

To pass properties to components, use **propsData** and not **props**. The latter is used to define properties, not to pass data.

First, create a **Message.test.js** file and add the following code:

```
describe("Message.test.js", () => {
  let cmp;

  describe("Properties", () => {
    // @TODO
  });
});
```

We group test cases within a **describe** expression, and they can be nested. So, we can use this strategy to group the tests for properties and events separately.

Then, we'll create a helper factory function to create a message component, and give it some properties:

```
const createCmp = propsData => mount(Message, { propsData });
```

Testing Property Existence

The most obvious thing that we can test is whether or not a property exists. Remember that the **Message.vue** component has a **message** property, so let's assume it receives that property correctly. vue-test-utils comes with a **hasProp(prop, value)** function, which is very handy for this case:

```
it("has a message property", () => {
  cmp = createCmp({ message: "hey" });
  expect(cmp.hasProp("message", "hey")).toBeTruthy();
});
```

Properties behave in such a way that they will only be received if they're declared in the component. This means that if we pass a **property that is not defined, then it won't be received**. Therefore, to check for the non-existence of a property, you could use a non-existing property:

```
it("has no cat property", () => {
  cmp = createCmp({ cat: "hey" });
  expect(cmp.hasProp("cat", "hey")).toBeFalsy();
});
```

However, in this case, the test will fail because Vue has **non-props attributes** (https://vuejs.org/v2/guide/components.html#Non-Prop-Attributes). This sets it to the root of the **Message** component, thus being recognized as a prop, so the test will then return **true**. Changing it to **toBeTruty** will make it pass for this example:

```
it("has no cat property", () => {
  cmp = createCmp({ cat: "hey" });
  expect(cmp.hasProp("cat", "hey")).toBeTruthy();
});
```

We can test the **default value** as well. Go to **Message.vue** and change the **props** as follows:

```
props: {
  message: String,
  author: {
    type: String,
    default: 'Paco'
  }
},
```

Then, the test could be as follows:

```
it("Paco is the default author", () => {
  cmp = createCmp({ message: "hey" });
  expect(cmp.hasProp("author", "Paco")).toBeTruthy();
});
```

Asserting Properties Validation

Properties can have validation rules, ensuring that a property is required or that it is of a determined type. Let's write the **message** property as follows:

```
props: {
  message: {
    type: String,
    required: true,
    validator: message => message.length > 1
  }
}
```

Going further, you could use custom constructors types or custom validation rules, as you can see in **the documentation** (https://vuejs.org/v2/guide/components. html#Prop-Validation). Don't do this right now; I'm just showing it as an example:

```
class Message {}

props: {
  message: {
    type: Message, // It's compared using instance of
    ...
    }
  }
}
```

Whenever a validation rule is not fulfilled, Vue shows a **console.error**. For example, for **createCmp({ message: 1 })**, the error would be as follows:

```
[Vue warn]: Invalid prop: type check failed for prop "message". Expected
String, got Number.
(found in <Root>)
```

At the time of writing, **vue-test-utils** doesn't have a utility to test this. We could use **jest.spyOn** to test it instead:

```
it("message is of type string", () => {
  let spy = jest.spyOn(console, "error");
  cmp = createCmp({ message: 1 });
  expect(spy).toBeCalledWith(
    expect.stringContaining("[Vue warn]: Invalid prop")
  );

  spy.mockReset(); // or mockRestore() to completely remove the mock
});
```

Here, we're spying on the **console.error** function, and checking that it shows a message containing a specific string. This is not an ideal way to check it since we're spying on global objects and relying on side effects.

Fortunately, there is an easier way to do it, which is by checking **vm.$options**. Here's where Vue stores the component options expanded. By expanded, I mean that you can define your properties in different ways:

```
props: ["message"];

// or

props: {
  message: String;
}

// or

props: {
  message: {
    type: String;
  }
}
```

But they all will end up in the most expanded object form (such as the last one). So, if we check the **cmp.vm.$option.props.message** for the first case, they all will be in **{ type: X }** format (although, for the first example, it will be **{ type: null}**).

With this in mind, we could write a test suite to test that the **message** property has the expected validation rules:

```
describe('Message.test.js', () => {
  ...
  describe('Properties', () => {
    ...
    describe('Validation', () => {
      const message = createCmp().vm.$options.props.message

      it('message is of type string', () => {
       expect(message.type).toBe(String)
      })

      it('message is required', () => {
        expect(message.required).toBeTruthy()
```

```
  })

  it('message has at least length 2', () => {
    expect(message.validator && message.validator('a')).toBeFalsy()
    expect(message.validator && message.validator('aa')).toBeTruthy()
  })
})
```

Custom Events

We can test at least two things in custom events:

- Asserting that an event gets triggered after an action

- Checking that an event listener calls when it gets triggered

This, in the case of the MessageList.vue and Message.vue components example, gets translated to the following:

- Assert that the Message components trigger a message-clicked when a message is clicked.

- Check MessageList to ensure that when a message-clicked is triggered, a handleMessageClick function is called

First, go to Message.vue and use $emit to trigger that custom event:

```
<template>
  <li
    style="margin-top: 10px"
    class="message"
    @click="handleClick">
      {{message}}
  </li>
</template>

<script>
export default {
```

```
    name: "Message",
    props: ["message"],
    methods: {
      handleClick() {
        this.$emit("message-clicked", this.message)
      }
    }
};
</script>
```

Then, in **MessageList.vue**, handle the event using **@message-clicked**:

```
<template>
  <ul>
    <Message
      @message-clicked="handleMessageClick"
      :message="message"
      v-for="message in messages"
      :key="message"/>
  </ul>
</template>

<script>
import Message from "./Message";

export default {
  name: "MessageList",
  props: ["messages"],
  methods: {
    handleMessageClick(message) {
      console.log(message)
    }
  },
  components: {
    Message
  }
};
</script>
```

Now it's time to write a unit test. Create a nested **describe** within the **test/Message.spec.js** file and prepare the bare bones of the "*Assert that the* **Message** *components trigger a* **message-clicked** *when a message gets clicked*" that we mentioned before:

```
describe("Message.test.js", () => {
  describe("Events", () => {
    beforeEach(() => {
      cmp = createCmp({ message: "Cat" });
    });

    it("calls handleClick when click on message", () => {
      // @TODO
    });
  });
});
```

Testing that the Event Click Calls a Method Handler

The first thing we can test is that when clicking a message, the **handleClick** function gets called. For that, we can use a **trigger** of the wrapper component, and a Jest spy using the **spyOn** function:

```
it("calls handleClick when click on message", () => {
  const spy = spyOn(cmp.vm, "handleClick");
  cmp.update(); // Forces to re-render, applying changes on template

  const el = cmp.find(".message").trigger("click");
  expect(cmp.vm.handleClick).toBeCalled();
});
```

See the **cmp.update()**. When we change things that are used in the template – **handleClick**, in this case – and we want the template to apply the changes, we need to use the **update** function.

Bear in mind that, by using a spy, the original **handleClick** method will be called. You will probably intentionally want that; however, normally, we want to avoid it and just check that on click, the method is indeed called. For that, we can use a Jest Mock function:

```
it("calls handleClick when click on message", () => {
  cmp.vm.handleClick = jest.fn();
  cmp.update();

  const el = cmp.find(".message").trigger("click");
  expect(cmp.vm.handleClick).toBeCalled();
});
```

Here, we're totally replacing the **handleClick** method, which is accessible on the **vm** of the wrapper component returned by the **mount** function.

We can make it even easier by using the **setMethods** helper that the official tools provide us with:

```
it("calls handleClick when click on message", () => {
  const stub = jest.spy();
  cmp.setMethods({ handleClick: stub });
  cmp.update();

  const el = cmp.find(".message").trigger("click");
  expect(stub).toBeCalled();
});
```

Using **setMethods** is the suggested way to do it, since it is an abstraction that official tools give us in case the Vue internals change.

Testing that the Custom Event message-clicked Is Emitted

We've tested that the click method calls its handler, but we haven't tested whether the handler emits the **message-clicked** event itself. We can directly call the **handleClick** method, and use a Jest Mock function in combination with the Vue **vm $on** method:

```
it("triggers a message-clicked event when a handleClick method is called", () =>
{
  const stub = jest.fn();
  cmp.vm.$on("message-clicked", stub);
  cmp.vm.handleClick();

  expect(stub).toBeCalledWith("Cat");
});
```

See that, here, we're using **toBeCalledWith**, so we can assert exactly which parameters we expect, making the test even more robust. That's not to say we're not using **cmp.update()** here since we're making no changes that need to propagate to the template.

Testing that @message-clicked Triggers an Event

For custom events, we cannot use the **trigger** method, since it's just for DOM events. However, we can emit the event ourselves, by getting the **Message** component and using its **vm.$emit** method. So, add the following test to **MessageList.test.js**:

```
it("Calls handleMessageClick when @message-click happens", () => {
  const stub = jest.fn();
  cmp.setMethods({ handleMessageClick: stub });
  cmp.update();

  const el = cmp.find(Message).vm.$emit("message-clicked", "cat");
  expect(stub).toBeCalledWith("cat");
});
```

I'll leave it up to you to test what **handleMessageClicked** does.

Wrapping Up

In this chapter, we've explored several cases of testing properties and events. **vue-test-utils**, the official Vue testing tool, makes this much easier indeed.

You can find the working code we've used here on **GitHub** (https://github.com/alexjoverm/vue-testing-series/tree/Test-Properties-and-Custom-Events-in-Vue-js-Components-with-Jest).

5

Test Computed Properties and Watchers

Computed properties and watchers are the reactive parts of the logic of Vue.js components. They each serve totally different purposes, that is, one is synchronous and the other is asynchronous, which makes them behave slightly differently.

In this chapter, we'll go through the process of testing them, and we'll see what different cases we can find along the way.

Computed Properties

Computed properties are simple reactive functions that return data in another form. They behave exactly like the language-standard **get/set** properties:

```
class X {
  get fullName() {
    return `${this.name} ${this.surname}`;
```

```
    }

    set fullName(value) {
      // ...
    }
  }
```

When you're using plain objects, then it'd be as follows:

```
export default {
  computed: {
    fullName() {
      return `${this.name} ${this.surname}`;
    }
  }
};
```

You can even add the **set** property as follows:

```
export default {
  computed: {
    fullName: {
      get() {
        return `${this.name} ${this.surname}`;
      },
      set(value) {
        // ...
      }
    }
  }
};
```

Testing Computed Properties

Testing a computed property is very simple. Sometimes, you probably won't test a computed property exclusively, but instead, you'll test it as part of other tests. However, most of the time it's good to have a test for it; whether that computed property is cleaning up an input or combining data, we want to make sure things work as intended. So, let's begin.

First of all, create a **Form.vue** component:

```
<template>
  <div>
    <form>
      <input type="text" v-model="inputValue">
      <span class="reversed">{{ reversedInput }}</span>
    </form>
  </div>
</template>

<script>
export default {
  props: ["reversed"],
  data: () => ({
    inputValue: ""
  }),
  computed: {
    reversedInput() {
      return this.reversed ?
        this.inputValue.split("").reverse().join("") :
        this.inputValue;
    }
  }
};
</script>
```

It will show an input and, next to it, you'll see the same string but reversed. It's just a silly example, but enough to test it.

Now, add it to **App.vue**, then put it after the **MessageList** component, and remember to import it and include it within the **components** component option. Then, create a **test/ Form.test.js** file with the usual bare bones we've used in other tests:

```
import { shallowMount } from "@vue/test-utils";
import Form from "../src/components/Form";

describe("Form.test.js", () => {
  let cmp;

  beforeEach(() => {
```

```
      cmp = shallowMount(Form);
    });
  });
```

Now, create a test suite with two test cases:

```
describe("Properties", () => {
  it("returns the string in normal order if reversed property is not true", ()
=> {
    cmp.setData({ inputValue: "Yoo" });
    expect(cmp.vm.reversedInput).toBe("Yoo");
  });

  it("returns the reversed string if reversed property is true", () => {
    cmp.setData({ inputValue: "Yoo" });
    cmp.setProps({ reversed: true });
    expect(cmp.vm.reversedInput).toBe("ooY");
  });
});
```

We can access the component instance within `cmp.vm` so that we can access the internal state, computed properties, and methods. Then, to test it is just about changing the value and making sure it returns the same string when **reversed** is **false**.

For the second case, it is almost the same, with the only difference being that we must set the **reversed** property to **true**. We could navigate through `cmp.vm...` to change it, but **vue-test-utils** give us a helper method, `setProps({ property: value, ... })`, that makes it very easy.

That's it; depending on the computed property, it may need more test cases.

Watchers

Honestly, I haven't come across any test case where I really need to use watchers that my computed properties couldn't solve. I've seen them misused as well, leading to a very unclear data workflow among components and messing everything up. So, don't rush into using them, and think beforehand.

As you can see in the **Vue.js docs** (https://vuejs.org/v2/guide/computed. html#Watchers), watchers are often used to react to data changes and perform asynchronous operations, such as performing an ajax request.

Testing Watchers

Let's say that we want to do something when the **inputValue** from the state change. We could perform an ajax request, but since that's more complicated (and we'll cover it in more detail in the next lesson), let's just use a **console.log function**. Add a **watch** property to the **Form.vue** component options:

```
watch: {
  inputValue(newVal, oldVal) {
    if (newVal.trim().length && newVal !== oldVal) {
      console.log(newVal)
    }
  }
}
```

Notice the **inputValue** watch function matches the state variable name. By convention, Vue will look it up in both the **properties** and **data** states by using the watch function name, in this case, **inputValue**, and since it will find it in **data**, it will add the watcher there.

Note that a watch function takes the new value as the first parameter and the old one as the second. In this case, we've chosen to log only when it's not empty and the values are different. Usually, we'd like to write a test for each case, depending on the time you have and how critical that code is.

So, what should we test about the watch function? Well, that's something we'll also discuss further in the next lesson when we talk about testing methods, but let's say we just want to know that it calls **console.log** when it should. So, let's add the bare-bones of the Watchers test suite within **Form.test.js**, as follows:

```
describe("Form.test.js", () => {
  let cmp;

  describe("Watchers - inputValue", () => {
    let spy;

    beforeAll(() => {
      spy = jest.spyOn(console, "log");
    });

    afterEach(() => {
      spy.mockClear();
```

```
      });

      it("is not called if value is empty (trimmed)", () => {
        // TODO
      });

      it("is not called if values are the same", () => {
        // TODO
      });

      it("is called with the new value in other cases", () => {
        // TODO
      });
    });
  });
```

Here, we're using a spy on the **console.log** method, initializing it before starting any test, and then resetting its state after each of them so that they start from a clean spy.

To test a watch function, we just need to change the value of what's being watched, in this case, the **inputValue** state. But there is something curious... let's start from the last test:

```
  it("is called with the new value in other cases", () => {
    cmp.vm.inputValue = "foo";
    expect(spy).toBeCalled();
  });
```

Here, we changed the **inputValue**, so the **console.log** spy should be called, right? Well, it won't. But wait, there is an explanation for this: unlike computed properties, watchers are *deferred to the next update cycle* that Vue uses to look for changes. So, basically, what's happening here is that **console.log** is indeed called, but after the test has finished.

Notice that we're changing **inputValue** in the *raw* way by accessing the **vm** property. If we wanted to do it this way, we'd need to use the **vm.$nextTick** (https://vuejs.org/v2/api/#vm-nextTick) function to defer code to the next update cycle:

```
  it("is called with the new value in other cases", done => {
    cmp.vm.inputValue = "foo";
    cmp.vm.$nextTick(() => {
      expect(spy).toBeCalled();
```

```
      done();
    });
  });
```

Notice here that we called a **done** *function that we received as a parameter. That's* **one way** **Jest** (https://jestjs.io/docs/en/asynchronous.html) *can test asynchronous code.*

However, there is a **much better way**. The methods that `vue-test-utils` give us, such as `emitted` or `setData`, take care of that under the hood. This means that the last test can be written in a cleaner way just by using `setData`:

```
it("is called with the new value in other cases", () => {
  cmp.setData({ inputValue: "foo" });
  expect(spy).toBeCalled();
});
```

We can also apply the same strategy for the next one, with the only difference being that the spy shouldn't be called:

```
it("is not called if value is empty (trimmed)", () => {
  cmp.setData({ inputValue: "    " });
  expect(spy).not.toBeCalled();
});
```

Finally, testing that it *is not called if the values are the same* is a bit more complex. The default internal state is empty; so, first, we need to change it, wait for the next tick, then clear the mock to reset the call count, and change it again. Then, after the second tick, we can check the spy and finish the test.

This would be much simpler if we recreated the component at the beginning, overriding the **data** property. Remember, we can override any component option by using the second parameter of the `mount` or `shallowMount` functions:

```
it("is not called if values are the same", () => {
  cmp = shallowMount(Form, {
    data: () => ({ inputValue: "foo" })
  });
  cmp.setData({ inputValue: "foo" });
  expect(spy).not.toBeCalled();
});
```

Wrapping Up

In this chapter, you've learned how to test part of the logic of Vue components: computed properties and watchers. We've gone through different example test cases that we could come across while testing both of them. You've also learned about some of the Vue internals, such as the **nextTick** update cycle.

You can find the code for this chapter on **GitHub** (https://github.com/alexjoverm/vue-testing-series/tree/Test-State-Computed-Properties-and-Methods-in-Vue-js-Components-with-Jest).

Test Methods and Mock Dependencies

What should we test in methods? That's a question that we had when we started doing unit tests. Everything comes down to *testing what that method does and only that*. This means we need to *avoid calls to any dependency*, so we'll need to mock them.

Let's add a **submit** event to the form in the **Form.vue** component that we created in the previous chapter:

```
<form @submit.prevent="onSubmit(inputValue)"></form>
```

The **.prevent** modifier is just a convenient way to call **event.preventDefault()** so that it doesn't reload the page. Now, make some modifications to call an API, and then store the result by adding a **results** array to the data as well as an **onSubmit** method:

```
export default {
  data: () => ({
```

```
        inputValue: "",
        results: []
    }),
    methods: {
      onSubmit(value) {
        axios
          .get("https://jsonplaceholder.typicode.com/posts?q=" + value)
          .then(results => {
            this.results = results.data;
          });
      }
    }
  };
```

Here, the method is using **axios** to perform an HTTP call to the **posts** endpoint of **jsonplaceholder**, which is just a RESTful API for this kind of example. Additionally, with the **q** query parameter, we can search for posts using the **value** provided as a parameter.

For testing the **onSubmit** method:

- We don't want to call **axios.get** actual method.

- We want to check it is calling axios (but not the real one) and that it returns a **promise**.

- That **promise** callback should set **this.results** to the promised result.

This is probably one of the hardest things to test when you have external dependencies, plus those return promises that do things inside. What we need to do is to **mock the external dependencies**.

Mocking External Module Dependencies

Jest provides a really great mocking system that allows you to mock everything in quite a convenient way. In fact, you don't need any extra libraries to do it. We have seen already **jest.spyOn** and **jest.fn** for spying and creating stub functions, although that's not enough for this case.

Here, we need to mock the whole **axios** module. That's where **jest.mock** comes into play. It allows us to easily mock module dependencies by writing at the top of your file:

```
  jest.mock("dependency-path", implementationFunction);
```

You must know that **jest.mock** is *hoisted*, which means it will be placed at the top:

```
jest.mock("something", jest.fn);
import foo from "bar";
// ...
```

So, the preceding code is equivalent to this:

```
import foo from "bar";
jest.mock("something", jest.fn); // this will end up above all imports and
everything
// ...
```

At the time of writing, I still haven't found much information about how to do in Jest what we're going to do here on the internet. Luckily, you don't have to go through the same struggle.

Let's write the mock for **axios** at the top of the **Form.test.js** test file and the corresponding test case:

```
jest.mock("axios", () => ({
  get: jest.fn()
}));

import { shallowMount } from "@vue/test-utils";
import Form from "../src/components/Form";
import axios from "axios"; // axios here is the mock from above!

// ...

it("Calls axios.get", () => {
  cmp.vm.onSubmit("an");
  expect(axios.get).toBeCalledWith(
    "https://jsonplaceholder.typicode.com/posts?q=an"
  );
});
```

This is great. We're indeed mocking **axios**, so the original axios is not called and neither is any HTTP called. And we're even checking, by using **toBeCalledWith**, that it's been called with the correct parameters. However, we're still missing something: *we're not checking whether it returns a* **promise**.

First, we need to make our mocked **axios.get** method to return a **promise**. **jest.fn** accepts a factory function as a parameter, so we can use it to define its implementation:

```
jest.mock("axios", () => ({
  get: jest.fn(() => Promise.resolve({ data: 3 }))
}));
```

However, we still cannot access the **promise** because we're not returning it. In testing, it is a good practice to return something from a function when possible, as it makes testing much easier. So, let's now do this in the **onSubmit** method of the **Form.vue** component:

```
export default {
  methods: {
    // ...
    onSubmit(value) {
      const getPromise = axios.get(
        "https://jsonplaceholder.typicode.com/posts?q=" + value
      );

      getPromise.then(results => {
        this.results = results.data;
      });

      return getPromise;
    }
  }
};
```

Then, we can use the very clean ES2017 **async/await** syntax in the test to check the promise result:

```
it("Calls axios.get and checks promise result", async () => {
  const result = await cmp.vm.onSubmit("an");

  expect(result).toEqual({ data: [3] });
  expect(cmp.vm.results).toEqual([3]);
  expect(axios.get).toBeCalledWith(
    "https://jsonplaceholder.typicode.com/posts?q=an"
  );
});
```

Here, you can see that we don't just check the promised result, but also that the `results` internal state of the component is updated, as expected, by doing `expect(cmp.vm.results).toEqual([3])`.

Keeping Mocks Externalized

Jest allows us to have all our mocks separated into their own JavaScript file by placing them under a `__mocks__` folder and keeping the tests as clean as possible.

So, we can take the `jest.mock...` block from the top of the `Form.test.js` file out to its own file:

```
// test/__mocks__/axios.js
module.exports = {
  get: jest.fn(() => Promise.resolve({ data: [3] }))
};
```

Just like this, and with no extra effort, Jest automatically applies the mock in all our tests so that we don't have to do anything extra, or manually mock it in every test. Notice that the module name must match the filename. If you run the tests again, they should still pass.

Keep in mind that the modules registry and the mocks state are kept as they are, so, if you write another test afterward, you may get undesirable results:

```
it("Calls axios.get", async () => {
  const result = await cmp.vm.onSubmit("an");

  expect(result).toEqual({ data: [3] });
  expect(cmp.vm.results).toEqual([3]);
  expect(axios.get).toBeCalledWith(
    "https://jsonplaceholder.typicode.com/posts?q=an"
  );
});

it("Axios should not be called here", () => {
  expect(axios.get).toBeCalledWith(
    "https://jsonplaceholder.typicode.com/posts?q=an"
  );
});
```

The second test should fail, but it doesn't. That's because **axios.get** was called on the test before.

For that reason, it's good practice to clean the module registry and the mocks, since they're manipulated by Jest in order to make mocking happen. For that, you can add in your **beforeEach**:

```
beforeEach(() => {
  cmp = shallowMount(Form);
  jest.resetModules();
  jest.clearAllMocks();
});
```

This will ensure that each test starts with clean mocks and modules, as it should be in unit testing.

Wrapping Up

The Jest mocking feature, along with snapshot testing, are the two things I love most about Jest. That's because they make what is usually quite hard to test very easy, allowing you to focus on writing faster and better-isolated tests and keeping your code base bulletproof.

You can find all the code for this chapter on **GitHub** (https://github.com/alexjoverm/vue-testing-series/tree/Test-State-Computed-Properties-and-Methods-in-Vue-js-Components-with-Jest).

Test Vue.js Slots

Slots are a means of making content distribution happen in the world of web components. Vue.js slots are made in accordance with the **Web Component specs** (https://github.com/w3c/webcomponents/blob/gh-pages/proposals/Slots-Proposal. md), meaning that if you learn how to use them in Vue.js, they will be useful moving forward.

They make the structures of components much more flexible, moving the responsibility of managing state to the parent component. For example, we can have a **List** component, and different kinds of item components, such as **ListItem** and **ListItemImage**. These will be used as follows:

```
<template>
  <List>
    <ListItem :someProp="someValue" />
    <ListItem :someProp="someValue" />
```

```
        <ListItemImage :image="imageUrl" :someProp="someValue" />
    </List>
</template>
```

The inner content of **List** is the slot itself, and it is accessible via the **<slot>** tag. Hence, the **List** implementation appears as follows:

```
<template>
    <ul>
        <!-- slot here will equal to what's inside <List> -->
        <slot></slot>
    </ul>
</template>
```

Now, let's say that the **ListItem** component looks like this:

```
<template>
    <li> {{ someProp }} </li>
</template>
```

Then, the final result rendered by Vue.js would be:

```
<ul>
    <li> someValue </li>
    <li> someValue </li>
    <li> someValue </li> <!-- assume the same implementation for ListItemImage -->
</ul>
```

Making MessageList Slot-Based

Now, let's take a look at the **MessageList.vue** component:

```
<template>
    <ul>
        <Message
            @message-clicked="handleMessageClick"
            :message="message"
            v-for="message in messages"
            :key="message"/>
    </ul>
</template>
```

MessageList has *hardcoded* the **Message** component inside. In one way, that is more automated but, in another, it is lacking in any flexibility whatsoever. What if you want to have different types of **Message** components? What about changing their structure or styling? That's where slots come in handy.

Let's now change **Message.vue** to use slots. First, move the **<Message...** part to the **App. vue** component, along with the **handleMessageClick** method, so that it's used externally:

```
<template>
  <div id="app">
    <MessageList>
      <Message
        @message-clicked="handleMessageClick"
        :message="message"
        v-for="message in messages"
        :key="message"/>
    </MessageList>
  </div>
</template>

<script>
import MessageList from "./components/MessageList";
import Message from "./components/Message";

export default {
  name: "app",
  data: () => ({ messages: ["Hey John", "Howdy Paco"] }),
  methods: {
    handleMessageClick(message) {
      console.log(message);
    }
  },
  components: {
    MessageList,
    Message
  }
};
</script>
```

Don't forget to import the **Message** component and add it to the **components** option in **App.vue**.

Then, in **MessageList.vue**, we can remove the references to **Message**. This now appears as follows:

```
<template>
  <ul class="list-messages">
```

```
    <slot></slot>
  </ul>
</template>

<script>
export default {
  name: "MessageList"
};
</script>
```

$children and $slots

Vue components have two instance variables that are useful for accessing slots:

- **$children**: An array of Vue component instances of the default slot

- **$slots**: An object of VNodes mapping all the slots defined in the component instance

The **$slots** object has more data available. In fact, **$children** is just a portion of the **$slots** variable that could be accessed the same way by mapping over the **$slots**. **default** array, filtered by Vue component instances:

```
const children = this.$slots.default
  .map(vnode => vnode.componentInstance)
  .filter(cmp => !!cmp);
```

Testing Slots

The aspect of slots that we probably want to test the most is where they end up in the component, and for that, we can reuse the skills we learned in *Chapter 3, Test Styles and Structure of Vue.js Components in Jest.*

Right now, most of the tests in **MessageList.test.js** will fail, so let's remove them all (or comment them out), and focus on slot testing.

One thing we can test is to make sure that the **Message** components end up within a **ul** element with the **list-messages** class. In order to pass slots to the **MessageList** component, we can use the **slots** property of the **options** object of the **mount** or **shallowMount** methods. So, let's create a **beforeEach** method (https://jestjs.io/docs/en/api.html#beforeeachfn-timeout) with the following code:

```
beforeEach(() => {
  cmp = shallowMount(MessageList, {
    slots: {
      default: '<div class="fake-msg"></div>'
```

```
      }
    });
  });
```

Since we just want to test whether the messages are rendered, we can search for **<div class="fake-msg"></div>** as follows:

```
it("Messages are inserted in a ul.list-messages element", () => {
  const list = cmp.find("ul.list-messages");
  expect(list.findAll(".fake-msg").length).toBe(1);
});
```

And that should be good to go. The slots option also accepts a component declaration, and even an array, so we could write the following:

```
import AnyComponent from "anycomponent";

shallowMount(MessageList, {
  slots: {
    default: AnyComponent // or [AnyComponent, AnyComponent]
  }
});
```

The problem with this is that it is very limited; you cannot override props for example, and we need that for the **Message** component since it has a required property. This should affect the cases that you really need to test slots with the expected components; for example, if you want to make sure that **MessageList** expects only **Message** components as slots. That's on track and, at some point, it will land in **vue-test-utils** (https://github.com/vuejs/vue-test-utils/issues/41#issue-255235880).

As a workaround, we can accomplish that by using a **render function** (https://vuejs.org/v2/guide/render-function.html). Consequently, we can rewrite the test to be more specific:

```
beforeEach(() => {
  const messageWrapper = {
    render(h) {
      return h(Message, { props: { message: "hey" } });
    }
  };

  cmp = shallowMount(MessageList, {
    slots: {
      default: messageWrapper
    }
```

```
    });
  });

  it("Messages are inserted in a MessageList component", () => {
    const list = cmp.find(MessageList);
    expect(list.find(Message).isVueInstance()).toBe(true);
  });
```

Testing Named Slots

The unnamed slot we used previously is called the *default slot*, but we can have multiple slots by using named slots. Let's now add a header to the **MessageList.vue** component:

```
<template>
  <div>
    <header class="list-header">
      <slot name="header">
        This is a default header
      </slot>
    </header>
    <ul class="list-messages">
      <slot></slot>
    </ul>
  </div>
</template>
```

By using **<slot name="header">**, we're defining another slot for the header. You can see the **This is a default header** text inside the slot. This is displayed as the default content when a slot is not passed to the component, and that's applicable to the default slot.

Then, from **App.vue**, we can add a header to the **MessageList** component by using the **slot="header"** attribute:

```
<template>
  <div id="app">
    <MessageList>
      <header slot="header">
        Awesome header
      </header>
      <Message
```

```
        @message-clicked="handleMessageClick"
        :message="message"
        v-for="message in messages"
        :key="message"/>
    </MessageList>
  </div>
</template>
```

It's now time to write a unit test for it. Testing named slots is just like testing a default slot; the same dynamics apply. So, we can start by verifying that the header slot is rendered within the **<header class="list-header">** element, and that it renders default text when no header slot is passed by. In **MessageList.test.js**, we have the following:

```
it("Header slot renders a default header text", () => {
  const header = cmp.find(".list-header");
  expect(header.text().trim()).toBe("This is a default header");
});
```

Then, the same but checking the default content gets replaced when we mock the **header** slot:

```
it("Header slot is rendered withing .list-header", () => {
  const component = shallowMount(MessageList, {
    slots: {
      header: "<div>What an awesome header</div>"
    }
  });

  const header = component.find(".list-header");
  expect(header.text().trim()).toBe("What an awesome header");
});
```

We can see that the header slot used in this last test is wrapped in a **<div>**. It's important that slots are wrapped in an HTML tag, otherwise **vue-test-utils** will complain.

Testing Contextual Slot Specs

We have tested how and where the slots render, and that's probably the most important aspect. However, it doesn't end there. If you pass component instances as slots, just as we're doing in the default slot with **Message**, you can test the functionality related to them.

Be careful as to what you test here. This is probably something you don't need to do in most cases since the functional tests of a component should belong to that component test. When talking about testing the functionality of slots, we test how a slot must behave *in the context of the component where that slot is used*, and this is something that is not very common. Normally, we just pass the slot and forget about it. So, don't get too attached to the following example – its sole purpose is to demonstrate how the tool works.

Let's say that, for whatever reason, in the context of the **MessageList** component, all the **Message** components must have a length of higher than 5. We can test this as follows:

```
it("Message length is higher than 5", () => {
  const messages = cmp.findAll(Message);
  messages.wrappers.forEach(c => {
    expect(c.vm.message.length).toBeGreaterThan(5);
  });
});
```

findAll returns an object containing an array of **wrappers** where we can access its **vm** component instance property. This test will fail because the message has a length of 3, so go to the **beforeEach** function and make it longer:

```
beforeEach(() => {
  const messageWrapper = {
    render(h) {
      return h(Message, { props: { message: "hey yo" } });
    }
  };
});
```

Then, it should pass.

Wrapping Up

Testing slots is quite simple. Normally, we'd like to test that they're placed and rendered as we want, so it is just like testing style and structure, knowing how slots behave or can be mocked. You won't need to test slot functionality very often in all probability.

Keep in mind that you should only test things related to slots when you want to test slots and think twice about whether what you're testing belongs to the slot test or the component test itself.

You can find the code relating to this chapter on **GitHub** (https://github.com/alexjoverm/vue-testing-series/tree/test-slots).

8

Enhance Jest Configuration with Module Aliases

The module managers that we have in the JavaScript community, primarily ES Modules and CommonJS, don't support project-based paths. They only support relative paths for our own modules and paths for the **node_modules** folder. As a project grows a little, it's common to see paths such as the following:

```
import SomeComponent from "../../../../components/SomeComponent";
```

Luckily, we have different ways to cope with this, in a way that we can define aliases for folders relative to the project root, so we can write the previous line as follows:

```
import SomeComponent from "@/components/SomeComponent";
```

Here, **@** is an arbitrary character to define the root project. You can define your own, however. Let's see what solutions we have available to apply module aliasing. Let's begin from where we left off in the **last chapter** (https://github.com/alexjoverm/vue-testing-series/tree/test-slots).

Webpack Aliases

Webpack aliases (https://webpack.js.org/configuration/resolve/#resolve-alias) are very simple to set up. You just need to add a **resolve.alias** property to your webpack configuration. If you take a look at **build/webpack.base.conf.js**, it already has it defined:

```
module.exports = {
  // ...
  resolve: {
    extensions: [".js", ".vue", ".json"],
    alias: {
      vue$: "vue/dist/vue.esm.js"
    }
  }
};
```

Taking this as an entry point, we can add a simple alias that points to the **src** folder and use that as the root:

```
module.exports = {
  // ...
  resolve: {
    extensions: [".js", ".vue", ".json"],
    alias: {
      vue$: "vue/dist/vue.esm.js",
      "@": path.join(__dirname, "..", "src")
    }
  }
};
```

With this alone, we can access anything, taking the root project as the **@** symbol. Let's go to **src/App.vue** and change the reference to those two components:

```
import MessageList from "@/components/MessageList";
import Message from "@/components/Message";
// ...
```

And if we run **npm start** and open the browser at **localhost:8080**, that should work out of the box.

However, if we try to run the tests by running **npm t**, we'll see that Jest doesn't find the modules. We still haven't configured Jest to do this. Therefore, let's go to **package. json**, where the Jest config is located, and add **"@/([^\\.]*)$": "<rootDir>/src/$1"** to **moduleNameMapper**:

```
{
  "jest": {
    "moduleNameMapper": {
      "@(.*)$": "<rootDir>/src/$1",
      "^vue$": "vue/dist/vue.common.js"
    }
  }
}
```

Here is an explanation of the preceding code snippet:

- **@(.*)$**: Whatever starts with `@`, and continues with literally whatever (**(.*)$**) till the end of the string, grouping it by using the parenthesis.

- **<rootDir>/src/$1**: **<rootDir>** is a special Jest word, meaning the root directory. Then, we map it to **src** and, with **$1**, we append the whatever clause from the **(.*)** statement.

For example, **@/components/MessageList** will be mapped to **../src/components/ MessageList** when you're importing it from the **src** or **test** folders.

That's really it. Now, you can even update your **App.test.js** file to use the alias as well since it's usable from within the tests:

```
import { shallowMount } from "@vue/test-utils";
import App from "@/App";
// ...
```

Also, it will work for both **.vue** and **.js** files.

Multiple Aliases

Very often, multiple aliases are used for convenience, so instead of using just a single **@** to define your root folder, you use many. For example, let's say you have an **actions** folder and a **models** folder. If you create an alias for each one and then you move the folders around, you just need to change the aliases instead of updating all the references to it in the codebase. That's the power of module aliases – they make your codebase easier to maintain and cleaner.

Now, let's add a **components** alias to **build/webpack.base.conf.js**:

```
module.exports = {
  // ...
  resolve: {
    extensions: [".js", ".vue", ".json"],
    alias: {
      vue$: "vue/dist/vue.esm.js",
      "@": path.join(__dirname, "..", "src"),
      components: path.join(__dirname, "..", "src", "components")
    }
  }
};
```

Then, we just need to add it to the Jest configuration in **package.json** too:

```
{
  "jest": {
    "moduleNameMapper": {
      "@(.*)$": "<rootDir>/src/$1",
      "components(.*)$": "<rootDir>/src/components/$1",
      "^vue$": "vue/dist/vue.common.js"
    }
  }
}
```

It is as simple as that. Now, we can try it in **App.vue** to use both forms:

```
import MessageList from "components/MessageList";
import Message from "@/components/Message";
```

Stop and rerun the tests and that should work. You may also run **npm start** and try that.

Other Solutions

I've seen **babel-plugin-webpack-alias** (https://github.com/trayio/babel-plugin-webpack-alias), especially used for other testing frameworks such as **mocha** (https://mochajs.org/), which doesn't have a module mapper.

I haven't tried it myself since Jest already provides you with that, but if you have done so, or want to try, please share how it went.

Wrapping Up

Adding module aliases is very simple and can keep your code base much cleaner and easier to maintain. Jest also makes it very easy to define them; you just need to keep in sync with webpack aliases, and you can say bye-bye to dot-hell references.

You can find the working code relating to this chapter on **GitHub** (https://github.com/alexjoverm/vue-testing-series/tree/Enhance-Jest-configuration-with-Module-Aliases).

9

Snapshot Testing

So far, you've seen how you can test the structure, styles, methods, computed properties, events, watchers, and more of Vue.js components. And you've learned to do this by using a variety of techniques and methods.

But what if I tell you that you can test most of it by simply using snapshot testing?

You've already seen snapshot testing being used in *Chapter 1, Write the first Vue.js Component Unit Test in Jest* and *Chapter 2, Test Deeply Rendered Vue.js Components* but those chapters focused more on explaining shallow and deep rendering, so I haven't yet explained it in detail.

Snapshot testing is the technique of assertion by comparing two different outputs.

Think of it as something similar to the screenshot technique used in end-to-end tests to check regressions: the first test run takes a screenshot of a part of the screen (for instance, a button), and, from that moment on, all the following runs of the same test will compare a new screenshot with the original one. If they're the same, the test passes; otherwise, there is a regression.

Snapshot testing works in the same way, but instead of comparing images, it compares serializable output, such as JSON and HTML, or just strings.

Since Vue.js renders HTML, you can use snapshot testing to assert the rendered HTML, given different states of a component.

Rethinking in Snapshots

For this example, let's consider the following **ContactBox.vue** component:

```
<template>
  <div :class="{ selected: selected }" @click="handleClick">
    <p>{{ fullName }}</p>
  </div>
</template>

<script>
  export default {
    props: ["id", "name", "surname", "selected"],
    computed: {
      fullName() {
        return `${this.name} ${this.surname}`;
      }
    },
    methods: {
      handleClick() {
        this.$emit("contact-click", this.id);
      }
    }
  };
</script>
```

In this case, we can test several aspects of this component:

- **fullName** is the combination of **name** + **surname**.

- It has a **selected** class when the component is selected.

- It emits a **contact-click** event.

One way to create tests that validate these specifications would be to check everything separately – the classes attached to the DOM elements, the HTML structure, the computed properties, and the state.

As you've seen in other chapters, you could perform these tests as follows:

```
import { mount } from "vue-test-utils";
import ContactBox from "../src/components/ContactBox";

const createContactBox = (id, name, surname, selected) =>
  mount(ContactBox, {
    propsData: { id, name, surname, selected }
  });

describe("ContactBox.test.js", () => {
  it("fullName should be the combination of name + surname", () => {
    const cmp = createContactBox(0, "John", "Doe", false);
    expect(cmp.vm.fullName).toBe("John Doe");
  });

  it("should have a selected class when the selected prop is true", () => {
    const cmp = createContactBox(0, "John", "Doe", true);
    expect(cmp.classes()).toContain("selected");
  });

  it("should emit a contact-click event with its id when the component is
clicked", () => {
    const cmp = createContactBox(0, "John", "Doe", false);
    cmp.trigger("click");

    const payload = cmp.emitted("contact-click")[0][0];
    expect(payload).toBe(0);
  });
});
```

But now, let's think about how snapshot testing can help us here.

If you think about it, the component renders according to its state. Let's refer to this as the **rendering state**.

With snapshot testing, instead of worrying about checking for specific things, such as attributes, classes, methods, and computed properties, we can instead check the rendering state, as this is the projected result of the component state.

For this, you can use snapshot testing for the previous test as follows:

```
it("fullName should be the combination of name + surname", () => {
    const cmp = createContactBox(0, "John", "Doe", false);
    expect(cmp.element).toMatchSnapshot();
});
```

As you can see, instead of now checking things separately, I'm just asserting the snapshot of `cmp.element`, this being the rendered HTML of the component.

If you run the test suite now, a `ContactBox.test.js.snap` file should have been created and you'll see a message in the console output as well:

```
Snapshot Summary
 › 2 snapshots written in 1 test suite.

Test Suites: 4 passed, 4 total
Tests:       25 passed, 25 total
Snapshots:   2 added, 2 passed, 4 total
Time:        8.696s
Ran all test suites.
```

Figure 9.1

Let's analyze the snapshot generated:

```
// Jest Snapshot v1, https://goo.gl/fbAQLP

exports[
    `ContactBox.test.js fullName should be the combination of name + surname 1`
] = `
<div
  class=""
>
  <p>
    John Doe
  </p>
</div>
`;
```

The purpose of this test is to check that the computed property, **fullName**, combines both the name and surname, separated by a space. Looking at the snapshot, you can see that this is happening and that *John Doe* is there, so you may consider this test valid.

In the same way, you can write the second test using snapshot testing:

```
it("should have a selected class when the selected prop is true", () => {
    const cmp = createContactBox(0, "John", "Doe", true);
```

```
    expect(cmp.element).toMatchSnapshot();
  });
```

Notice that the only aspect that changes between this test and the previous one is the setting of the **selected** property to **true**.

That's the power of snapshot testing: you play with *different states of the components,* while you just need to assert the rendering state.

The purpose of this test is to validate that it has a **selected** class when the property is **true**. Now, let's run the test suite again, and if you check **ContactBox.test.js.snap** again, you'll see that another snapshot has been added:

```
exports[
  `ContactBox.test.js should have a selected class when the selected prop is
  true 1`
] = `
<div
  class="selected"
>
  <p>
    John Doe
  </p>
</div>
`;
```

And the selected class is there, as expected, so we can consider this one to also be valid.

When Snapshot Testing Doesn't Help

Have you noticed that I didn't mention anything about the third test? To recall this test, let's check it again:

```
it("should emit a contact-click with its id when the component is clicked", ()
=> {
  const cmp = createContactBox(0, "John", "Doe", false);
  cmp.trigger("click");

  const payload = cmp.emitted("contact-click")[0][0];
  expect(payload).toBe(0);
});
```

In this case, when the component is clicked, it doesn't perform any action that changes the component state, which means that the rendering state won't change. We're just testing behavior here that has no effect on the rendering of the component.

For that reason, we can say that *snapshot testing is useful for checking changes in the rendering state*. If the rendering state doesn't change, there is no way that snapshot testing can help us.

When a Test Fails

The snapshots generated are the source of truth when it comes to deciding whether a test is valid. That's the way regressions are checked, and, ultimately, that depends on your criteria.

For example, go to the `ContactBox.vue` component and change the `fullName` computed property to be separated by a comma:

```
fullName() {
  return `${this.name}, ${this.surname}`;
}
```

If you run the tests again, some of them will fail since the rendering result is different from before. You'll get an error along the lines of the following:

```
Received value does not match stored snapshot 1.

  - Snapshot
  + Received

    <div
      class=""
    >
      <p>
  -     John Doe
  +     John, Doe
      </p>
    </div>
```

From that point on, as it's usually in relation to testing, you must decide whether that's an intentional change or whether it's a regression. You can press 'u' in order to update the snapshots:

```
Snapshot Summary
 › 1 snapshot test failed in 1 test suite. Inspect your code changes or press `u` to
update them.

Test Suites: 1 failed, 1 total
Tests:       1 failed, 2 passed, 3 total
Snapshots:   1 failed, 1 passed, 2 total
Time:        0.99s, estimated 3s
Ran all test suites related to changed files.
```

Figure 9.2

It would be convenient when applying TDD to use the watch mode, `npm run test --watch`. This would be very convenient since Jest gives you a number of options for updating snapshots:

- Press '**u**' to update all snapshots.

- Press '**i**' to update snapshots interactively, one by one.

Conclusion

Snapshot testing **saves you a lot of time**. This example was basic, but imagine testing a more complex component with many different rendering states...

Sure, you can assert in relation to specific things, but that's much more cumbersome than asserting how the component is rendered depending on the state, since, most of the time, if you change the code, you have to change the assertions in relation to the tests, while, with snapshot testing, you don't need to.

Additionally, you can **find regressions** that you didn't take into account, perhaps something you didn't consider in your tests, or something that has changed the rendering of the component, but the snapshots will alert you to this.

I would now like to mention a number of **caveats** that you should remember:

- Snapshot testing doesn't replace specific assertions. While it can do so most of the time, both ways of testing are totally combinable.

- Don't update snapshots too easily. If you see that a test fails because it doesn't match a snapshot, take an in-depth look at it before updating it too quickly. I've been there as well.

If you want to try it yourself, you can find the full example used in this chapter on **GitHub** (https://github.com/alexjoverm/vue-testing-series/tree/chapter-9).

Index

About

All major keywords used in this book are captured alphabetically in this section. Each one is accompanied by the page number of where they appear.

Made in the USA
Middletown, DE
19 November 2020

24531621R00051